I0038958

CREATING A LOVE THAT LASTS

A MARRIAGE THAT'S STRONGER THAN SHATTERPROOF GLASS

KENNETH AND TONGELA SMITH

Creating a Love That Lasts:
A Marriage That's Stronger Than Shatterproof Glass
Copyright © 2020 Kenneth Smith / Joi Publishing

All rights reserved. No part of this book may be repro-
duced by any mechanical, photographic, or electronic
process, or in the form of phonographic recording; nor
may it be stored in a retrieval system, transmitted, or
otherwise copied for public or private use without the
prior written permission of the authors.
Send inquiries to creatingalovethatlast.com

Kenneth Smith / Tongela Smith.

ISBN 978-1-7361497-0-6 (Paperback)
ISBN 978-1-7361497-1-3 (Ebook)

Edited by Christine Bode
Book Cover Design by Trevor Bailey
Book Production by Dawn James, Publish and Promote
Design and Layout by Davor Nikolic

Printed and bound in the United States of America.

Note to the reader: The events in this book are based
on the authors' experiences and from their perspective.
The information is provided for educational purposes
only. In the event you use any of the information in this
book for yourself, which is your constitutional right, the
authors and publisher assume no responsibility for your
actions.

CONTENTS

FOREWORD

We can remember many years ago someone asked us to write a foreword to a book they had written on marriage. After reading the book, we found there were examples of struggles in marriage but no solutions - no victory. We questioned this and the response troubled us. We were asked, "Can anyone really be happy in marriage?" No doubt we were surprised but we realize there are so many couples like them that feel they are stuck in a relationship that has no hope of happiness but have learned to live with the struggles. Listen, we know it's not marriage that makes you happy but that our happiness comes from the Lord. Our victory is in Christ Jesus. "For whatsoever is born of God overcometh the world: and this is the victory that overcometh the world, even our faith." 1 John 5:4 KJV

There are biblical answers to all the struggles in marriage. If something is broken, take it to the one who made it. Our faith and trust must rest in God alone. He is the creator of the marriage covenant.

The world is in the middle of a coronavirus pandemic and other world disasters. There are other known pandemics and disasters that are taking place concurrently that we are unaware of, in relationships. There are viruses of distrust, insecurity, infidelity, hate, envy, strife, etc. Everyone dreams of the perfect relationship but unfortunately, those dreams do not always come true. Couples desire to create a love that lasts but don't know how and don't understand how to make a marriage work. In this must-read book, *Creating a Love That Lasts,* couples will discover the answers to having a healthy relationship, how to weather the storms that occur in life, and will discover the different phases that relationships can experience, and with this understanding, build a strong relationship and create a love that lasts.

We were so blessed to read *Creating a Love That Lasts* because it not only allowed us to reflect on our relationship but also on how these Apostles look at relationships within their ministry. We have counseled and married many couples over the years and believe that having this book as a foundation when entering into marriage, will help every couple create a love that lasts. There are many life lessons to discover that will help couples navigate their relationship to a good and healthy place. *Creating a Love That Lasts* gives us some of those life lessons.

That couple who wanted to help other married couples live with their struggles ended their relationship in divorce. That does not have to be your story. God has answers for every struggle. Your victory is in Jesus!

We would advise everyone to take the quiz in Chapter 6 to discover where you are in the phases of your relationship, as understanding where you are will help you discover where you need to be, and where you want to go. Start reading this book today and let it help you to get the most out of your relationship.

Romans 12:9-12 ERV states,
"Your love must be real. Hate what is evil. Do only what is good. Love each other in a way that makes you feel close like brothers and sisters. And give each other more honor than you give yourself. As you serve the Lord, work hard and don't be lazy. Be excited about serving him! Be happy because of the hope you have. Be patient when you have troubles. Pray all the time."

Apostles Tony and Cynthia Brazelton

ACKNOWLEDGEMENTS

First and foremost, all the glory to God our King! We dedicate this book to our four children, two son-in-laws, and grandchildren, who are a force of love and inspiration in all that we do.

Thank you to Pastor Burnard and Jessie Scott, and Bishop Reginald and Dr. Cynthia McGill for setting fine examples of a strong marriage.

To Naomi L.M. Booker for being the agent to re-unite us.

To Mom and Dad, and Tony and Cynthia Brazelton, our covering Apostles - thank you for your leadership and love.

Special thanks to Kellie Umstead for her incredible work in assisting us with this project.

INTRODUCTION

Finding one's true love has been the dominant fantasy of people throughout history. It is the essence of myths, movies, fairy tales, poetry, and love songs. Shrouded in this universal longing is the idea that there is one unique person who is "perfect for me" and in discovering that person, "I will live happily ever after." The person we desire as a life-long companion typically has a specific personality type. When we find that matching personality, we fall "hopelessly in love" and live in the illusion of happiness for a season.

Once the illusion of love fades, it becomes crystal clear that finding love is not a problem for many but keeping love and maintaining the connection is a prominent issue. The truth is, most couples are unaware that at this point, the relationship moves into a five-phase cycle that will forever characterize their attachment. Being ignorant and lacking the skills to recognize and manage the phases causes a power struggle to ensue, one in which many couples never recover.

Creating a Love That Lasts presents a model of the five phases that is easy to grasp and gives a deeper understanding of a relationship's inevitable conflicts. It will also help you to develop the skills needed to navigate the natural fluctuations of relationship seasons.

This book is for those on the brink of marital disaster; husbands and wives in a second marriage; people wanting to strengthen their happily married journey; lonely wives; browbeaten husbands; spouses in affairs; victims of relationships; engaged couples; divorcees in need of healing; and pastors or counselors looking for material that can save marriages.

Creating a Love That Lasts provides a road map to the mysterious, challenging, and wondrous journey of wholehearted love in a way that familiarizes you with the relationship life cycle. If you desire peace, miss having an intimate connection to your spouse, and long to feel understood, then *Creating a Love That Lasts* will provide the understanding you need to help normalize marital fluctuations and make better decisions during moments of intense fellowship. As you read this work, you'll find a framework and practical techniques for flowing through the five stages while remaining in sync with your spouse and developing greater intimacy.

We hope this book will offer you a deeper understanding of a relationship's inevitable conflicts, a reflective space in which to examine your own choices, and a guide to strengthen your connection with your mate. Finally, we hope that this book will serve as a reminder that intimate relationships are, most of all, an "inside job," and that no matter where you start, the destination is *Creating a Love That Lasts*.

CHAPTER 1

THE CONVERGE AND MERGE

Falling in love is one of the most surprisingly remarkable experiences we could ever have or know as our lives are immediately infused with new meaning, mystery, and fascination. The first phase of a relationship consists of a converge and merge where boundaries melt away, and a sense of "we-ness" is all there is. Our similarities and differences thrill us, no matter how odd or vague. We both wanted a chocolate Labrador Retriever. We both loved the same song in the ninth grade, and we both agree that Androids are better than iPhones. During the Converge and Merge phase, everything becomes evidence that we are perfect for each other and destined to be together forever.

The onset of love is a transcendent experience with a sacredness that allows us to peer deeply into the other's spirit. Just as important, our inner light seems to shine brighter than we could have ever imagined. We idealize our partner as merely marvelous, and we notice the grandest part of ourselves as well. We not only listen carefully, but we hang on every word that our new love interest says, and we seem to only give the ideal and best response. Our enthusiasm for them is boundless, and our patience is eternal. The largeness of our spirit and the potency of our generation can be observed from miles away. It is indeed a delight to live with an open heart, endless possibilities, unconditional love, care, and abundant joy.

We go on to create a love bubble, a world where only we exist and float in pure happiness forever. This feeling engulfs us, but is not sustainable, as eventually the bubble bursts and we must find our way back to ourselves.

Melvin and Kim

Kim is a successful health-care administrator, sharp and elegant. Melvin, a pediatrician, is tall and lanky with a warm and gentle nature that instantly puts people at ease. Together, they make a beautiful couple.

The two met during a hospital staff meeting. Initially, Kim saw the typical doctor, accomplished, self-satisfied, even a tad arrogant. However, Melvin knew that he had a heart as well as a brain, and a well-developed ego. He was also compassionate, which was evident as he instituted an animal-assisted therapy program at the hospital so that seriously ill children could cuddle and play with dogs and bring in their pets as well.

Having to be around children quite a bit, Melvin also had a well-developed inner clown. He had a habit of wearing the goofiest neckties that endeared him to his sick, pint-sized patients. Melvin noted that his comical ways impressed Kim as she one day commented, "I wish every doctor had your sense of play and fun."

In the following weeks, the two were magnetically drawn to each other. Melvin's charm and kindness for children impressed Kim. Her directness and confidence impressed him. Melvin put effort into making sure every encounter with her was filled with zany humor. This stirred something within him as he was raised in an impersonal and stoic family. For the first time in her life, Kim felt nurtured, very much like the children under his care.

Melvin asked Kim to join him for afternoon coffee and she gladly accepted. This led to lunches in the hospital cafeteria, followed by weekend concerts and dinners, which led to passionate evenings at their homes. The excitement broke through the barriers she'd erected as an upper-class member of society in Virginia. The woman who was formerly thought of as an ice queen now acted more like a schoolgirl. As she listened to Melvin tell stories about growing up on a Minnesota farm, she felt enthralled by the simplicity of his upbringing. With every conversation, outing, and every moment spent together, Kim felt herself unfold and surrender.

And Melvin? He initially judged Kim as unapproach-able and dismissed her as highbrow, too sophisticated for his Minnesota simplicity. He'd overheard her con-versations about having season tickets to the opera and her experiences at the top luxurious private spas in the city. There was, however, a vivaciousness about her that intrigued him. By the time Melvin approached Kim, his perspective had changed quite a bit. He had become more cultured, traveled to many parts of the world, and finally gained enough confidence to believe that he may have a chance with this cultured woman who had intimidated him in the past. Her ice queen reputation at the hospital no longer scared him off but heightened his interest.

When Kim agreed to have coffee with him, he was elated. As they drank coffee together and he looked into her deep brown eyes, he saw his soul reflected there. There was no doubt in his mind that she was the one for him and that they would build a life together.

Yielding to Romance

During the initial phase of love, our emotional brain assaults our rational mind until it yields to romance. Caution and fear melt away, and we submit to the gratification of romance. The fight between the desire to converge and merge and the need to remain an individual is finally won by knockout in the first round; individuality didn't stand a chance in the ring of Converge and Merge! And into the love bubble, we go, creating our own private culture. We invent a new language of our own that no one else can comprehend. We share jokes that no one else would find the least bit funny. The Converge and Merge has occurred, and we feel safe, total, and eternal.

This was the case with film star Ingrid Bergman and her husband, Petter Lindström. The two had a daughter and named her Pia, with the three letters standing for Petter, Ingrid, Always. Of course, their marriage dissolved, but Pia's name was a constant reminder of the love they once shared – both its possibilities and its fragilities.

Now, we must mention that not every couple experiences the urge to converge and merge. Some experience a hit of ecstasy that quickly vanishes, and some never feel it at all. Some experience a gradual love that leads to an intimate partnership – one that may or may not be spiced with romance. Others simply make a choice because of the accelerating ticking of the biological clock or the perceived ability to enter new circles of influence that may have a positive impact on their professional positioning and career goals. For many, it has nothing to do with love but merely following cultural expectations. Nonetheless, so much of our culture – fairy tales, songs, movies, novels – leads us to believe that we must pursue the princess who will cater to our every need and melt our heart, or that we must seek the prince who will dissolve our angst and provide all the security we could ever want with a kiss.

A Kind of Madness

The Converge and Merge phase is filled with a kind of madness. We fantasize about our beloved throughout the day and cling to them at night. When we're apart, we long for them. We have a preoccupation that others find initially delightful, and later quite nauseating.

A new couple has much in common with gamblers and other addicts. Magnetic resonance images have shown that parts of the brain light up when people are genuinely in love in very much the same way that parts of the brain light up in cocaine users as they indulge in their addiction.

Long-Lasting Love Requires Work

Falling in love is just as it sounds, the effortless toppling of oneself. However, long-lasting love is the result of two people doing the necessary self-work that creates a robust and durable partnership that lasts for years. The work is not easy and is more likely to succeed if we've wisely chosen a compatible partner. This, my friend, is the obstacle. The strength of the romantic feelings experienced during Converge and Merge does not guarantee that our love object is a great partner for us. This is why many people sober up only to realize that their intended lacks emotional maturity or is a hurtful narcissist who is incapable of creating room for two as he or she is distracted by his or her own glory. Choosing well is a task not for the weak, especially since we are biochemically and psychologically wired to select a specific type of mate.

Harville Hendrix and Helen Hunt are the co-creators of Imago Relationship Therapy. Years of research confirms that the time of Converge and Merge provides a type of anesthesia that sometimes makes us oblivious to the notion that the person we are choosing is incompatible. According to Hendrix and Hunt, every person carries an Imago of an inner image of the traits of our primary caregivers. The traits are found to be a combination of the best and worst. If we had a parent who was overcritical or even narcissistic, we find ourselves unwittingly seeking those same characteristics in a mate. The soul tends to choose based on who will help it to continue, as a means of safety or to resolve emotional challenges that linger from childhood. Therefore, the soul wants a partner who demonstrates the very qualities that challenge him or her.

Kim chooses Melvin because his silliness is the quality she was raised to deny, and deep down, she desires to resolve the anger she feels in having to suppress that playfulness that she vehemently wanted to express as a child. Melvin chooses Kim because she embodies the mixed reactions he received about his excessive humor while growing up. They are both gravitating towards the soul that has the potential to help heal the wounds.

The good news is while there are bio-psychological reasons for choosing a partner, we can also control our reasoning for selecting a mate. We can pay attention to our love interest's level of self-awareness and integrity and investigate their relational history. We can note whether they ever acknowledge the part they play in situations, no matter how seemingly small, or whether they tend to play the blame game. How people handle various cases and opportunities for communication helps us to understand how they will handle them in the future.

The Path to a Happier Life

Learning to love deeply and well is one of the supreme achievements of life. According to the 2017 publication, Dialogues in Clinical Neuroscience [19(1)9-19], love strengthens our immune system, develops our heart and organ functions, and alters our brain pathways. Love has the potential to unlock humanity's most significant potential. The journey on this path, however, isn't comfortable and is one of life's most challenging endeavors. When love knocks on the door of our hearts, and we invite it in, we succumb to the false belief that we will forever be saved from disappointment and loneliness. Instead, we have only accepted an invitation to know disappointment and loneliness in a way that we would not have chosen and would never have imagined.

As we emerge from the Converge and Merge, we have hopefully matured with less emphasis on fleeting satisfaction. We are now more fully equipped to delight in our significant other while standing firm in our own space and being. Indeed, the stage of Converge and Merge has brought sweetness to our lives that can be equated to the sweet-smelling fragrance of a well-cultivated rose garden in the spring. But now we must travel through the next three phases – Distrust and Denial, Disillusionment, and Decision – before we reach the final phase, Creating a Love That Lasts.

The expedition through love's five phases helps us to embrace the fact that while love is never-ending, it also changes. The nature of love mirrors the various aspects of life itself in all its loveliness. It encompasses the weather patterns that include thunderstorms, hurricanes, tornados, rain, hailstorms, droughts, and sunshine. To have a love that lasts, we must accept that these are all things that will occur over the lifetime of the marriage or relationship. When we realize that healing does not come from preventing these conditions, but through accepting them as part of the very essence of love and making room for them to occur, we allow our relationship to blossom, and we are empowered to reclaim the best of our individual and collective selves.

CHAPTER 2

DISTRUST AND DENIAL

This must happen. Eventually, we experience the restrictiveness of the cocoon we've built for two. We begin to miss our independence, our former pleasures, the company, and the comfort of our friends and family. We crave time for ourselves and want to have fun with others. The characteristics that we found so heartwarming about our love interest begins to irritate us. Her liveliness now seems insincere and annoying – *no one is that happy all the time,* you think. His controlled demeanor and dependability are now viewed as boredom and rigidity. Suddenly, the person we loved so dearly isn't as enjoyable as we thought. We start to wonder if we're right for each other at all.

We have spasms and pinches of doubt, which become a waltz of sorts. We ebb and flow, spinning around to push away the uncertainty and deny its existence. We're on alert for negative or disagreeable things that our partner says, and we twirl away at the first sign of alarm. However, we quickly suppress these feelings through denial, and tap-dance our way back to "the way things were."

Just as tap dancing involves improvisation and reinterpretation, we reimagine our first and second arguments as a testament. Many of us do this tap dance exceedingly well – we reinterpret our first fight as evidence that our love can overcome any obstacle. We manage to support the notion that all is well and blissful. Since we characterize it as joyful, we don't discuss any details of the argument as we believe it was only a minor upset to what is truly a perfect partnership.

Although this is our story that we choose to stick to, it is a sign that the love bubble has popped, and we are on the way to being confronted with the differences that have been there all along. Not only will these differences confront us, but they will soon begin to slap us repeatedly in the face until we, at last, admit that our love isn't perfect. Soon, we begin to attack and criticize, and we also realize that the one we loved so dearly finds fault with our behavior, too.

What once was a glorious, rapture experience has now turned into a disappointing catastrophe. Love blinded us, and we didn't see this realization coming.

The truth is we are distinct people with distinct needs that will never wholly converge and merge. Where our heart once sang, "welcome," it now cries, "beware." The oxytocin and endorphins that once flooded our system have given way to stress hormones that give rise to fight and flight. The eternal romantic in us has been traded for the street fighter.

If we are not careful, we find ourselves in an infinite loop that works like this: I fear rejection and find out that you fear intimacy, which causes you to push me away. As you withdraw, your detached stance causes me to feel abandoned. As my anxiety sets in, I attempt to break through to you and draw you closer. You, in turn, disengage, and the cycle repeats over and over.

Oh, No, We're Different!

When the second phase is underway, we recognize differences in the way we see the world, differences in spending and saving habits, social needs and desires, movies, hobbies, sports, and books that we enjoy. And if this isn't enough, we discover what we believe may be the worst difference of all, contrasting sexual desires.

We must remember that the first phase is so exuberant and exciting that someone with a naturally low libido may experience a temporary elevation. However, once that initial step is circuited through, some find it difficult to be aroused, which may then lead to a similar cycle of frustration, rejection, withdrawal, abandonment, and anxiety, as described in the previous passages above.

In creating a love that lasts, couples must understand that these shifts in behavior are quite regular. There is nothing wrong with us. The widespread misconceptions about love are that the couple will always have a fulfilling sex life and have equal desire and pleasure if they both genuinely love each other. *This is simply not true.*

Those with a high propensity for sexual intimacy will ponder sex more often and may be attracted to others. Those with less of a need for sexual intimacy will think of sex less and have less of a desire to be intimate. The tragedy of not knowing this truth is that both succumb to a level of frustration and rejection and conclude that they are no longer loved or attractive to their mate. Ultimately, this becomes yet another indication of their incompatibility. We believe if we had chosen better, we would not have the experience of this eroding relationship.

To top it all off, our culture is laced with images of undying passion and perfect relationships that mirror the likes of Prince William and Kate Middleton or Prince Harry and Meghan Markle. Ultimately, the imagery around us leads to conflicted feelings and thoughts about our partner that not only is our relationship off somehow, but it is doomed.

Learning to Navigate

Creating a love that lasts means realizing that nothing makes us more vulnerable to being the most susceptible, behaving the most reactive, and receiving our deepest wounds than being in a relationship. However, when we decide to learn the necessary skills and tools, we don't have to give in to the fight or flight stress response. We can learn to navigate through difficulties in ways that cause us to move closer to and deepen our capacity for genuine, enduring love.

One of the things engaged couples and those who desire to enter a lasting relationship need to understand is that two people who have lived separately for the majority of their lives will naturally have two points of view on how to live life together. They may differ on simple things such as the type of music to play in the car while driving to church, which charity to volunteer at or donate funds to, or where to vacation. Different perspectives on personal hygiene, eating habits, or sleeping habits may also rise – not to mention which side of the family to spend holidays with or which political candidate to vote for. To heighten our emotions, these differences may emerge during a conflict.

Since many have not practiced collaborating during a conflict, this may lead to contention, disapproval, defiance, strife, and worst of all, the desire to give up.

The strategy we use depends on personal experiences, family history, spiritual beliefs, and personality quirks. Those who tend to withdraw will disappear for a season. An avoider will deny that there is a problem or try to please their way out. A confrontational person will fight to win. While these are natural responses, none of them are very conducive to collaboration.

CHAPTER 3

DISILLUSIONMENT

I magine a toddler experiencing the "terrible twos" – as we have so characterized this phase of development – due to their curious and exploratory nature. Toddlers need to assert themselves yet remain connected. You notice your toddler is quiet. You go into the living room and find your bundle of joy throwing about the DVDs that he has just liberated from the entertainment center. You are greatly angered and attempt to remove him from the mess, which prompts him to scream at the top of his lungs and flail his arms wildly in the air. As you tidy up the mess he's made, he crawls off to discover what else he can get into, in a nearby corner. The next thing you know, he crawls back to you and clings to your leg, hoping you will pick him up for a cuddle.

The third phase of love, Disillusionment, is very much like what we've experienced with toddlers. The truth is the terrible twos weren't so awful. There was simply a tension between the competing desires of freedom and connection that toddlers find quite irritating and unsettling; hence the wailing, yelling tantrums in childhood. Now, as adults, the same frustration troubles and envelops us during the phase of Disillusionment. Of course, this time around, we do our best to act maturely, but our success is usually partial at best. The tension between growing and developing individually and fostering a relationship is the beginning of a dark, wintry season of love.

Love's Frosty Interval

The power struggle seems quite formidable like a winter blizzard boasting whiteout conditions. The passion that once characterized the relationship has wholly vanished among the wintry conditions that cover and bury everything in its path. Emotional distance turns into a thick, icy glaze that you dare not travel upon, with no timeline for thawing and melting away in sight. The repetitive arguments have worn us out entirely, and to maintain the thin thread of connection, we decide to endure this phase quietly in our separate quarters of the house.

The doubts and distance feel so incredibly real and even final. Distance is only one way this stage is handled. Some act out dramatically and even violently. No matter how it is expressed, this phase is common in all relationships and is merely a part of a cycle. Amid the pain and distress, however, it is a strain to understand that Disillusionment is a natural phase of love. It helps to view this phase, like all five phases, as a gift that has come to develop us individually and as a couple. We only need to stop our ranting and pouting long enough to find the courage and patience to discover the gift.

The ongoing assignment of love is two-fold. One, as many of us know, is to learn to unconditionally love another. The other assignment is generally overlooked, but is even more critical, which is to learn to love ourselves. The self-love I'm referring to is not vain and selfish, nourished by money, power, and influence. Instead, it is a type of physical, mental, and spiritual self-care; one that frees us to foster, discover, rediscover, and redefine gifts, talents, and life purpose.

We all know from safety demonstrations performed on every airline flight that in the event of an emergency, we must put our mask on first before helping anyone, even a defenseless child. This best reminds us of love's paradox: as we take care of ourselves and feel good about who we are, we are more likely to take care of and feel generous towards our mate and others. This is the basis of creating a love that lasts. As we take care of our needs, we feel centered, safe, and open enough to risk acknowledging our shortcomings and partnering, wholeheartedly. The inner critic that would interfere and assault our sense of self gives way to a deep understanding of worthiness that allows us to make apologies, and to expect and provide care and respect.

The "I" Factor

If you recall, the first phase, Converge and Merge, was all about the glorious illusion of oneness. In phase two, Distrust and Denial caused a brief panic as we realized that we are two separate individuals, but we comfortably settled back into the cocoon of "we." Now, in the third phase, there is no clinging to fantasy as this time of profound disenchantment causes us to abandon the idea of "we" and run into the arms of the perceived safety of "I". We've discovered that our differences are substantial, aggravating, and permanent. Creating a love that lasts means taking care of ourselves and acknowledging that to become all that we can be, we must integrate the "I" and the "We".

The previous generation valued marital longevity as the ultimate goal. It didn't matter if you were miserable as long as you hung in there. If you were a reasonably happy and healthy unit and had financial security, that was the icing on the cake. Today, the number one marker of marital success is emotional fulfillment and long-lived intimacy with our partner. Wow, how times have changed! Yet we can only share this type of relationship if we first have it or are open to developing it within ourselves.

The gift of the Disillusionment phase is that the romantic aphrodisiac has worn off, so we are free to take an honest look at ourselves and develop a vision and a goal for the love and respect we deserve and desire to freely give. If we never encountered this stage, the love and respect we seek would never become possible because we would never enter a stage that provides the privilege to candidly look at ourselves. The first two phases would blind us to the faults of our mate. Seeing the mistakes of our mate and experiencing the seesawing of the heart allows us to look inward and later gain a balanced view of ourselves, our mate, and the two of us as a unit.

The Slob and the Domestic Police

Let us revisit Kim and Melvin. They are now twelve years into their relationship. Kim and Melvin married and seem to have had many years of wedded bliss. They are parenting ten-year-old twins and have made their home in an affluent suburb in Ohio.

The pair are known to be pillars of the community and fixtures of the major charity events. The problem is that beneath the near-perfect exterior, the couple has been at war for the last six months. The country upbringing Melvin experienced used to fascinate Kim, and now she finds the habits he learned during his childhood to be quite uncivilized and tacky. While she still enjoys his wacky humor in the privacy of their own home, she wishes he had sense enough to conceal it in public. As a result, once they arrive at posh social events, she immediately scurries off to find her friends, as she cannot bear to watch him embarrass himself to no end. Her contempt for him is typically something she never scurries away from as she often rolls her eyes and puts him down at dinners with friends. Melvin finds her insults disrespectful, but he never protests aloud.

He knows he is an intelligent, well-informed man who has a desire to let loose sometimes. What is wrong with that? Melvin notices more and more that she never released her stodgy upbringing after all these years, and as the years passed, he finds her attachment to status to be more and more repulsive. He often feels like Kim's mother has invaded her body as he witnesses her rude treatment of waiters, salesclerks, and other service people. Like her father, Kim constantly name-dropsy. Anyone they come in contact with is immediately given her educational pedigree, which includes her parents, graduates of Yale, and her MBA from Harvard. *Give it a rest,* Melvin often thinks to himself.

Their home life has become the ultimate battlefront. Kim is now a vegan and arrogantly snubs Melvin's need for meat at every meal. She forbids him to use anything but red pots to cook his meat dishes as she does not want his immoral eating habits to taint her natural lifestyle. Of course, Melvin will conveniently forget (more like ignore) her requirements that she has expressly marked "for use by carnivores." He is also more and more annoyed as she cuts up her food into tiny fragments and measures everything she eats. He feels that controlling her diet in this way is ridiculous, and what disturbs him, even more, is the tendency Kim has, to control everything in the household.

The TV can only be watched at a specific volume. The children have to stick to eating at specific times from a special menu of food. He thinks of her more as the family police than his wife. There are non-stop activities for the children: music lessons, homework, and each is active in three sports that gobble up their time. Even their unstructured playtime is regimented. He resents that the twins are barred from experiencing the wonder and freedom of childhood that characterized his youth.

Meanwhile, Kim believes her life is perfect in terms of her children, career, and community influence. The only problem that she wishes she could rid herself of is her poor choice of husband. *What a slob,* she often thinks as he leaves tiny whiskers on his bathroom sink after shaving. He doesn't have the appreciation she has for fine dining and continuously makes the dumbest jokes to the guests and waitresses.

The two pretty much hate the sight of each other and rely more and more on their social activities to pull them through the dreadful relationship they have built. The little time that they spend alone at home is in silence or the occasional reminder about the children's activities. Their sex life is nonexistent, and on the rare occasion that they do indulge, it is very robotic and quick.

The Point of No Return

During the spring of this year, Melvin's brother visits. One morning they decide to go fishing. As Melvin and his brother enjoy the peace and quiet out on the calm waters, his anger and disappointment creep up on him. He begins to recount to his brother all the nasty comments, the overbearing and controlling rituals, and the misery he has endured over the past several years. Suddenly, he utters to his brother, "Marrying

Kim has been the biggest mistake of my life. It's time to face facts and call the marriage what it is – over."

Instantly a wave of freedom rushes over him, and the tightness that he's felt around his throat for years is gone. He begins to speak of a time when he could enjoy his kids apart from Kim and her perpetual nagging. He would finally be able to cook in whatever pot he desired. Astoundingly, he realizes with confidence that the best solution is to simply start a new life without her.

CHAPTER 4

DECISION

Melvin had reached the place that many of us are familiar with – the hard, unyielding place where we conclude that our only option is to permanently escape the insufferable ways of our spouse. It seems as if there is no other way forward, and we have reached the fourth phase of love – Decision.

This phase is defined by exhaustion that is incomprehensible. We've taken all the disappointment we can take, and a feeling of desperation to escape characterizes every aspect of life. It's time to release the pent-up anger, break loose from that insufferable partner, and make a new start.

For years we have worked with couples who are in this phase. This tends to be the only phase when couples reach out to us. We can't tell you how many times over the years we have uttered the following sentences:

1. You should not take phase four as an immediate impulse to leave unless you are in danger.
2. If you are, then move out and on, immediately.
3. If you do not stop and ask yourself these essential questions before you take the next step, it is because truthfully, you have not reached the ending but only a crossroads to a new beginning, together.

For most couples, the fourth phase seems like the end, but it is decision time, and yet another gift if it can be perceived as such. The Decision phase is a platform on which to rest, contemplate your choices, gain new insight, and possibly launch yourself and your spouse into a new, more exhilarating existence than you ever thought possible. It is the optimal time for renewal and growth. Falling in love is effortless, which is why we call it "falling" in love and not working our way into love or some other phrase that would indicate exertion. The beauty of the Decision phase is that we're exhausted, we've reached the end of ourselves, and we're ready to wake up. In the fourth phase, it's not the decision you make that is most important, but *how* you make the decision that will change your life and the life of your family unit forever.

Although a decision is now required of us, the irony is that most of us are not in the frame of mind to make the right decision about the future of our relationship. Again, our old friend tension enters. The tension in phase four relates to the conflicting urges that whisper in our ear, *it's impossible to stay,* and *it's saddening to leave.*

What do we do with this ambivalence?

The main thing we do not want to do is make an irreversible decision at this point. What's interesting is that during our careers, we review and revise contracts, goals, mission statements, and job descriptions yearly, but we never think to do the same with relational goals, missions, and specifications. We expect them to remain the same year after year. However, our relational contracts deserve to be reviewed by couples with introspection and reflection. This is a time to courageously consider your mistakes and regrets. It is time to reevaluate your needs and desires. This will leave you better equipped to assess your options and make the best decision about your relationship. What you can learn about yourself in this stage will serve you and your spouse well.

Options and Opportunities

The options that characterize the fourth phase are:
1. To separate.
2. Remain together in a state of conflict and in-difference.
3. Remain together and lead separate lives.
4. Rebuild and create a more wholesome and re-warding union.

We owe it to ourselves and our partners to explore our role in the conflict. This can lead to a new resilience, a new kind of bond. As we emerge from this phase, we will enter the Creating a Love That Lasts stage and then loop back to phase one, Converge and Merge. However, we will never return to the pure, idealistic dizzying passion that existed before. Instead, we will have created a healthier relationship that considers the past, embraces reality, and stretches to attain future possibility.

This sets the stage to move into the fifth phase, *Creating a Love That Lasts.*

CHAPTER 5

CREATING A LOVE THAT LASTS

During the first phase, love disarmed us. As we converged and merged with our partner, not only did we welcome vulnerability, but it felt effortless and natural. We accepted his peculiarities, supported his vision and ideas, shared many secrets, and were open to flirtation and passion. Since then, we've moved through Distrust and Denial, Disillusionment, and Decision – and although we may wish it possible, we can't go back the way we came.

A Couple on the Brink of Disaster

Most of us could sense that Melvin and Kim were on a surefire collision course. But what would happen next may have been beyond our imagination.

Melvin stopped on the way home from the hunting trip to buy Kim's favorite roses as a peace offering. Kim and the kids were not home when he arrived. Melvin placed the stunning bouquet of roses on the kitchen counter, imagining her eyes dancing as she walked in and saw the enormous long-stemmed bouquet. He had not bought a card but remembered there were cards upstairs in Kim's dresser drawer. Melvin eagerly ran upstairs, opened the drawer, and reached for the cards that were peeking from behind a folded piece of paper. As he picked up the box of cards, the paper opened and revealed a brief handwritten note signed by someone named Shane. It read like a love note.

Suddenly, it seemed as if the entire world stopped. Melvin felt like he had been kicked in the chest and immediately flopped on the bed in disbelief. He told himself not to think or overthink the situation as there had to be a reasonable explanation. After all, Kim would never do something so careless and selfish as this. Yet, he remained in one spot almost as if he were bolted to the bed.

An hour later, he heard the garage door open and the sound of the children and Kim walking into the house and getting settled. Melvin snapped out of the mindless stupor he had been in for the last hour and headed downstairs to greet his family. There in the kitchen stood Kim, admiring the huge vase of flowers.

Her hair was perfectly draped over her shoulders, and although she had been running around with the kids, her clothes were still perfectly placed as if she'd just gotten dressed. Kim turned in delightful surprise and thanked Melvin for the beautiful flower arrangement. "You're certainly welcome," Melvin replied, smiling. He thought it was annoying to have to plaster a fake smile on his face at a time like this.

Kim lightly kissed his forehead and began to tell him about the day. Melvin picked up his kids at the same time and hugged them as they giggled incessantly. He felt very robotic at the moment he went through the motions of welcoming everyone home. He wanted to bring up the note from Shane but also wanted to take in these last moments of civility before the bomb dropped on the family unit.

The next day, everyone went through their regular routines. Kim asked Melvin to pick up some fresh parsley and spinach on his way home from the hospital. As she walked toward the door leading to the garage, she even smacked him on the behind, which was something she hadn't done in years.

Melvin came home that evening empty-handed and offered a weary, "Sorry, I forgot," as he entered the kitchen and saw a sea of vegetables on the cutting board.

"You couldn't remember to do one thing. I only asked you to do one thing for me," Kim said in her typical disdainful tone.

Usually, Melvin would ignore her tone, but today it set him off. "Yet another rude reminder that I don't measure up to your standard of perfection," he exploded. "Everything about me annoys you. The clothes I wear, the way I relax and unwind, what I read, how I brush my teeth."

Kim simply ignored him, continuing to cut up the veggies, leaving him to his daily tantrum. She ate dinner at the table and Melvin ate dinner in front of the TV.

During a commercial break, Melvin said to her, "Let's face it, we are tired of each other."

"Gee, you think so, Einstein," she snapped back.

Melvin's rage took over, and he threw his plate on the kitchen floor near where Kim was sitting. "You're not as perfect and put together as you portray yourself to be."

"I have to be pretty close to perfect so that I can take care of the kids and manage the house, something you seem quite incapable of doing," Kim replied very calmly.

"And do you manage Shane as well?"

Kim's jaw dropped, and for the first time in years, she was speechless. Melvin stood there in silence, basking in the pleasure he felt at calling her out and for the first time in their relationship, she did not have an immediate and snappy reply.

"Yeah, I was looking for a card so I could write you a thoughtful love letter when I found a romantic note to you from Shane. How imperfect of you to not hide it better."

Kim didn't lose her cool at all, even in the face of the discovery of her dirty little secret being uncovered. "Okay. So now you know," she declared as she cleared the table and walked over to the dishwasher.

"I need you to be open and honest with me. Are you having an affair?"

"Not only am I having an affair, but I am in love with him," Kim stated while placing her plate in the dishwasher.

She had met Shane as she was picking up her son from a birthday party. He was the divorced father of one of their son's best friends.

"How could you?" Melvin hissed as he gritted his teeth.

Hearing his wife admit to cheating on him, so nonchalantly with the parent of their son's friend was an absolute horror to him. He wanted someone to pay and vacillated between who deserved more harm, Shane, or Kim. He felt flashes of heat run through him, and the intensity scared him. He ran upstairs, packed a suitcase, and headed out the door, for fear that he was going to do something he would regret.

War... No Peace

Melvin checked into a hotel, and over the next three days, he barely slept as he contemplated all the ways to do bodily harm to Kim and Shane. He called in sick for an entire week, ruining his perfect attendance record at work. Melvin didn't eat for five days straight and let his imagination run wild with details and images of Kim and Shane sharing laughs and moments of intimacy at his expense. He imagined slamming Shane's head into a wall. He decided he wanted to be present when Kim was served the divorce papers. These two thoughts were the only thoughts that gave him a sense of pleasure and relief.

He called his attorney to start the divorce process. The attorney spoke to Melvin's rational brain, warning him against any acts of violence he was considering. His attorney advised him to be mindful of the children in this process and how important it was to allow the law to work for him. Melvin knew that everything his attorney said was right, yet this inner storm raged on. Kim had managed to suck the life and happiness out of him. As he compared how in love they once were, and where they stood now, heartbreak flooded his psyche. He pounded on the wall, dropped down on his knees, and wept for what seemed like hours. Eventually, he crawled into bed, feeling the full weight of his exhaustion, and fell asleep.

Melvin woke up to the sound of his cell phone vibrating. It was Kim. She suggested that they find a therapist. Melvin was used to recommending psychotherapy when he saw signs of distress and depression in his patients but never imagined that he, too, would need a therapist. Where he came from, people sorted out their personal problems. In a state of desperation and exhaustion, he agreed that they should see a marriage counselor.

That evening he received a text from Kim that stated, "I want to work out our issues, Melvin. I really do." Melvin tossed the phone on the bed in disgust. The phone vibrated again, and he reluctantly picked it up and read the message, "Are you willing to try?"

After an hour of sitting there staring at the phone, Melvin replied, "I don't know if we can, Kim, so much has happened... but I am willing to try."

The next afternoon, Kim and Melvin strolled into the therapist's office with fake smiles and an air of togetherness. The therapist noted their posture and quickly cut through the tension by asking the couple what they wanted to accomplish.

Kim quickly blurted out, "I desperately want to save our marriage, but I don't know how."

"I want to go back to how our relationship was in the beginning when we were honest and faithful and filled with admiration for each other," Melvin chimed in.

"Frankly, this marriage is over," said the therapist. "The sooner you acknowledge it, the better off you will be." They were both alarmed by his statement.

"What? We aren't saying we want to end it," Kim relaxed into her calm and collected demeanor while Melvin remained speechless.

"I understand where you are," the therapist nodded. "However, to move forward, you must acknowledge that the previous relationship is over and done. But it doesn't mean that we can't create a new reality for the two of you. From this point forward, we'll work together to create a new, more resilient marriage."

Kim and Melvin met weekly over the next year, feeling intimidated and clueless most of the time. Their commitment was commendable. Kim disconnected from Shane and openly and honestly answered Melvin's questions about the relationship. Kim noted her growth as she took total responsibility for her choices and actions and never blamed Melvin. They were excited when they realized significant progress and were grateful for the miracle of a new beginning.

The therapist helped them unearth the roles they each played in the deterioration of their marriage. After roughly six months of therapy, they began to understand the breakdown and setbacks in their marriage and were now setting the scene for a fantastic comeback. They could see clearly how they had blocked the intimacy they both so desperately wanted and how their childhood deficits played a role in the collapse of the marriage. They even arrived at the place where they could laugh about their slipups. Most importantly, they realized the fragility that is part of the marriage unit; they understood that they would not always be able to give and receive love unconditionally and that they would not always agree with and please each other. They also realized that ironically this slump in their marriage had placed them on the road to achieving self-actualization.

Melvin realized that to forgive Kim for her indiscretion, he would have to work through his tendency to hold grudges and use them for a false sense of superiority.

They slowly but surely began to open their hearts and were well on their way to Creating a Love That Lasts.

The goal in this fifth phase – Creating a Love That Lasts – is to recapture the bliss of the initial phase without the help of the potent love elixir that once made everything so easy and effortless. The only way to regain some of the original zest and zeal of our early days together is to create an entirely new partnership – one that is grounded in unfaltering love.

This type of love is based on the awareness that our significant other cannot meet all our needs. The desperation associated with romantic love – the feelings of I can't do anything without you, and I need to make sure I do all that I can to make you love me and make you stay – melts away as the ever-present assurance that God has made us enough to embrace who we are and has equipped us with what we need to take care of ourselves with his help.

The realization that we can share and care without trying to fix each other, change each other, or make the other forever aware of our value has evaporated. In its place is only the agenda of responding to each other from the most mature, stable, honest, and energetic parts of ourselves.

Roadblocks Ahead

While there may be a few curbs on the journey to creating a love that lasts, the road is plain and straightforward. The only roadblocks we experience are the ones that we put in our way. The barriers we lay are meant to block our pain, but they block our joy as well. Since most of us are not aware enough to not lay them down, we must learn to dismantle them. This involves examining the fears and limitations that have emerged due to various life experiences. It means taking the obstacle and viewing it from a different angle and acknowledging with compassion why we erected the roadblock in the first place.

The Roadblock of Codependence

On the journey of creating a love that lasts, a common issue is the soul's enmeshment and entanglement or codependence, wherein we compromise our own needs and boundaries to suit him or her. In the process, we deny our truth and our brilliant existence to tranquilize each other with the hope that our partner will replenish us and become our life buoy.

Instead of codependence, we must maintain healthy boundaries:

- We must stick to our non-negotiables, trusting that they are set for a reason.
- We must be willing to cooperate with all other aspects of life with our partners.
- We must live in the space of knowing that we are all self-contained individuals who are brilliantly weaved with gifts and abilities that are all our own. It is only a privilege to make a mutually beneficial exchange.
- We must realize that our sense of self-worth, security, and well-being isn't tied exclusively to the ebb and flow of our relationship and that we possess the inner resources to be grounded within ourselves and tell the truth about what we need and who we are.

The only reason we are on the journey of creating a love that lasts is to become more aware of the wholeness that we already possess. We never need to change another person or to win their approval and love.

The Roadblock of Love Addiction

Fantasy love is very alluring and seductive. It is a distractor and detractor from pure love and the wholeness that already exists. The biochemical reflexes and responses we experience from fantasy love are hard to uproot. The object of your fantasy becomes an addiction as their love feels like your very salvation. It moves you to shred your boundaries and break your rules of engagement to please him or her. You will extinguish your own needs and preferences to ensure the most positive response.

The beauty of revolving through these five phases is that we form new thoughts and uncover unique skills that help us define love in a new way. We come to understand that our mate will not meet all our needs but will help us to understand what it means to love with all our hearts.

The Closed Heart Roadblock

When we experience loss, disappointment, or heartbreak, we tend to close up. This is the stuff our most beloved songs are made of because they speak to the universal sorrow of a broken heart! Remember hearing Tina Turner wail, "What's Love Got to Do with It?" Or how about Beyonce's "Irreplaceable," or Billy Ray Cyrus singing about his "Achy Breaky Heart"?

"The anger and hurt we feel changes our blood flow, alters our neurotransmitters, alters our taste for food, sense of smell, and other sensations."
~ *Louise B. Miller, Ph.D.*

Moving Toward Love's Summit

We've discussed the roadblocks we can manifest and have discovered the reasons we create them. Take time to consider some of your barriers and why they exist. Awareness becomes our best chance of vanquishing them and opening ourselves to the possibility of realizing love to its fullest.

When we first fall in love, it is as if we take a helicopter ride to the top of the Swiss Alps, viewing some of the most magnificent mountains in the world, overcome with wonder and delight. Eventually, we had to land and return to base camp where we were subject to slips, stumbles, falls, high winds, and the treacherous job of climbing the mountain, if we so chose. Just like Melvin and Kim, we had to decide whether the climb was worth the risk and consider the possible injuries we could sustain as we attempted to scale great heights. But as we continue to climb, we realize that we are fortifying ourselves and learning invaluable lessons.

The rewards become more and more worthwhile as we reach significant milestones in the ascent.

Bridges and Overpasses

Creating a love that lasts involves the development of new paradigms in which both partners are committed to the celebration of what already exists in the other. These are our bridges and overpasses that are built as we practice acceptance of our partners and ourselves. Instead of concrete, plaster, and steel, we use the spiritual virtues of compassion, patience, and gratitude to construct grand roads that take us from one place in life to another.

The Second Time Around

When we're in the fifth phase, we experience the connectivity that we felt in the first. However, there is a profound difference between the source and our intentions. In the fifth phase, there is little to no desperation. Ethical boundaries are in place, and we are comfortable with saying yes or no to requests.

It was psychologist and writer Sam Keen who said, we become wholehearted "not by finding a perfect person, but by learning to see an imperfect person perfectly." We can accept another's imperfections because we are reassured that we're whole and worthy of love.

The Bridge to Self-Worth

Kim and Melvin continued to do the work, uncovering the connections between their childhood scripts and their actions and reactions to each other. They gained a greater understanding of their family dynamics and were able to expand and experience new possibilities as they discovered their self-worth that had been buried through childhood experiences and pain. Both effectively bridged the gap between the past and present and founded a new transformative bond.

The Bridge to Generosity

The dopamine high of infatuation is no longer what moves us in the fifth phase. We are now free of old habits, love fantasies, and addictions that blind us to the beauty and greatness within us. Generous gestures are enough to spark a fire of passion. We may simply tell her what we appreciate most about her and ignite an eternal flame. Making a morning cup of coffee or tea for him, showing appreciation for ordinary things, and saving an article about something he cares about are examples of the superglue of generosity that holds relationships together.

This love even seeps through our relationship with our spouse and begins to massage close friends and family. It also has the propensity to affect those we have never met or may never respond to. The openness of our heart becomes a reservoir of prayer, practical action, and support as grace and tenderness radiate out in the world to those who need it most.

The Bridge to Play and Fun

You'll often hear "play" suggested for couples whose marriages are in trouble. This is because play tends to teach skills of cooperation and relieve stress. The problem is that most married people don't know how to be playful as it is often an attribute that is lost in our late twenties.

Play was suggested to Kim and Melvin. They had no idea how this would or should unfold in their marriage but decided that a vacation may be an excellent way to awaken their playful natures. They took a trip to Costa Rica and were present on the beach when a crew of leatherback turtles appeared from the sea, laying eggs on the beach in the moonlight. The experience of nature taking its course right before their eyes, in such a simple manner, sparked not only a feeling of affection and appreciation but an eagerness to become advocates for sea turtles. They decided to work together with an organization that was dedicated to this cause, and this sparked renewed love and care for each other.

The beginning of a relationship is typically filled with flirting and passions. These pleasures can continue and tend to become integrated with new, more profound, and shared intellectual interests, which is less typical during phase one. Since this is a significant gateway way to passion, consider purchasing tickets to an acrobatics performance, going for a hike, or inviting friends to dinner. These types of pursuits tend to be lighter, indirect methods for arousing fun, satisfaction, and romance. Many people don't consider these things because they are still stuck in phase one. But remember, each phase can help us to evolve and allow us a more fulfilling existence, so we must migrate to other phases for the growth of our passion and sexual intimacy.

The Overpass to Laughter

Nothing relieves tension, breaks down walls, awakens our energy, and brings a sense of closeness like humor.

Gerald had just lost his wife Contessa, after 15 years of marriage and seven years of battling cancer. To his surprise, his wife's death wasn't the dark, unbearable time he had imagined. As a couple, humor had always been an intricate part of their lives. Even during the worst parts of Contessa's illness, they would hold each other, cry together, and then abruptly start laughing at how intensely they were crying.

Initially, when Contessa died, Gerald felt lost and was truly broken-hearted. One evening a friend took him to a stand-up comedy club, and during one of the sessions, Gerald realized a great way to channel his grief. Six months after her death, Gerald decided to host an annual community comedy sketch in her honor. Each year, the event gained momentum, and he seemed to heal through the creative work of sharing with others something they always enjoyed – laughter and jokes.

Gerald ended each performance by reciting Psalm 30:11: "You turned my wailing into dancing," and every audience seemed to applaud loudly after Gerald recounted this verse, as it became a truly uplifting experience for the community. The way he expressed his grief is also reflected in an observation by Jewish Rabbi Baal Shem Tov, who was quoted as saying, "There are three ways to mourn – to weep, to be silent, and to sing."

A New Reality

After much struggle, Melvin and Kim recommitted to their marriage and constructed a new one. They both agreed that it was much better than even the initial years, typically referred to as marital bliss. To be clear, this does not mean that they rode off into the sunset, holding hands and gazing into each other's eyes. This is far from the truth.

Occasionally, Melvin still thought about the idea of Kim with another man and relived the feelings of betrayal that he felt when he first discovered it. At times, he also lingered in regret of the beauty of living on a farm and longed for the sights, scents, and sounds that could not be found in the suburban life they had built. He often chuckled to himself about the unlikely match they made. He never in a million years would have ever thought he'd be married to a sophisticated, high-brow woman like Kim, but admired the fact that he was because he never suffered from boredom. He found her quite an impressive specimen because of her sophisticated ways, for the rest of his life.

As for Kim, she bought two horses, as she was determined to integrate some of Melvin's passions into their suburban life. She enjoyed the times that she and Melvin ditched the crowded restaurants for a bit of country air and the sound of whinnying horses. However, make no mistake about it, Kim was still Kim and continued her season tickets to the opera and symphony. She no longer punished Melvin for wearing silly-looking ties around her friends and began to enjoy his outlandish humor almost as much as their friends did. Kim had moments of ambivalence when she would remember how cultured Shane was and wondered how his life was going as she had always admired that Shane understood and appreciated the more beautiful things in life.

The two came to a place where they realized the contrasts between their backgrounds did not define them as a couple, but it did create a space for appreciation of differences. They became kinder towards each other as they were fundamentally aware of the fragility that was embedded in the marriage. They found new ways to move together through life as playmates, partners, and friends who would weather the storms of life together. They had no intention of taking each other for granted again, primarily since they had invested immense amounts of time and energy into repairing their relationship.

They continued to cycle through the phases of Disillusionment, Converge and Merge, Distrust and Denial, and Decision. Sometimes they rode these waves anticipating what new thoughts and ideas would emerge as they surfed through them. There were other times when they wearied of the infinity loops and wanted to escape. But they always seemed to regain their composure and positive outlook as these cycles continue to produce better individuals who are capable of nourishing each other and highlight the wholeness that both bring to their relationship, children, friends, and community.

The Resident Gift

We are always rotating through these five relationship phases. We experience loops, shutdowns, hurts, and annoyances. We've heard about the stages of grief and how we can experience each stage for extended periods or circle through them rapidly within a matter of hours. It is the same with the phases of love and this is what is at the heart of creating a love that lasts.

To create a love that lasts, then, is to know we won't find ourselves in any one phase and stay there forever. Ironically, what highlights our wholeness and acceptance is always subject to change. But there is a resident gift we gain through the daily practice of love and willingness to journey through the phases. We no longer need and crave the glittery infatuation that was so prevalent during the first phase. We only need to be cognizant of the promise of love that will emerge as we traverse each phase and celebrate that this is the journey of a lifetime.

CHAPTER 6

DISCOVER THE STAGE OF LOVE YOU'RE IN

We're sure that as you've read through *Creating a Love That Lasts*, you've identified with the various relationship phases. We've created a simple quiz to help you understand what phase you're currently in. Knowing where you're at can help you effectively communicate, allow for space, and fully experience the freedom and lessons that come with each phase.

Here's how it works: using a scale of 1 to 10, rate how true each statement is for you. At the end of the quiz, you'll score yourself, and we will help you interpret your score.

This is only a mini quiz to get you started. For a full assessment of where you are in your marriage and how to make the most of it, we urge you to visit CreatingALoveThatLast.com and take the assessment there.

This relationship makes me feel amazing; it's like walking in sunshine and rainbows most of the time.

_____ The similarities and complementary nature of our interests, thoughts, and beliefs are quite astonishing.

_____ Our connection is genuinely spiritual.

_____ It's easy for us to talk for hours, only pausing to realize how fascinating we are together.

_____ We sleep close together, often keeping our arms around each other.

_____ We may have only been together for a short period, but I know that this is the perfect person for me.

_____ I like all the quirky habits, facial expressions, and unusual style of my partner. I could never imagine asking him/her to change a thing.

_____ When we're apart, I wonder what he/she is doing. I long to hear about his/her day.

_____ We find joy and fun in the most mundane activities, whether it's going to the grocery store, taking the car in for an oil change, or walking the dog.

_____ Some of the traits that I once found amusing or exciting in my partner are becoming a little annoying.

_____ He/she is beginning to criticize me and compare me to other people. It's very irritating, but if I'm honest, I sometimes do the same.

_____ The only time we sleep close together is if we are about to be intimate.

_____ There's no more sexual magic; I only pretend that there is.

_____ Every day I notice annoying habits and aggravating flaws. Why didn't I see them before?

_____ Am I failing at love once again? Will this work out?

_____ I'm tired of the arguments. A loving couple should not argue this much.

_____ I never had these issues with my family and friends. I miss the outings, activities, and friendships I enjoyed before this relationship.

_____ I desire the ease and effortless connection we used to have.

_____ Wow, I become more and more disappointed in my partner each time we interact. He/she is so different from the person I thought he/she was.

_____ Why do we argue about the same things over and over?

_____ I'm bored and bothered... PERIOD. My partner tells the same stories and jokes all the time. Please get some new material ASAP!

_____ I no longer feel I can share my real thoughts with my partner.

_____ We remain angry about things longer than we should. When we attempt to resolve our issues, it only leads to defensiveness.

_____ Our sex life sucks.

_____ I wish I had seen the visible troubling signs before we committed to one another.

_____ From now on, I want him to remain on his/her side of the bed and not touch me. I'm entirely turned off from him/her and do not need to reach to his/her side of the bed.

_____ I chose the wrong person and am considering moving on.

_____ Why did I ever think we were in love? This is not loving.

_____ We pretty much live separate lives, and that's completely fine with me.

_____ Why did I ever choose this person over the other options I had?

_____ This relationship is absolutely exhausting.

_____ The problems we face far outweigh the benefits of us being together.

_____ I want my old life back and constantly fantasize about separating.

_____ I don't want to go on like this. We're at a crossroads and it's time to decide to go in one direction or another.

_____ The stress of the relationship is affecting my health. My skin is breaking out. My blood pressure is elevated. I'm tired most of the time from worrying.

_____ I don't want to have to look at him/her anymore.

_____ I get more enjoyment from doing activities with friends and family than with my partner.

_____ It seems that our relationship is beyond repair. I can tell we're getting closer to the end.

_____ All is not lost. I believe there are things we can do to repair this relationship and make it great.

_____ I'm willing to have difficult conversations with my partner if that's what it takes. I'm eager to communicate differently.

_____ I feel like I can be myself with my partner.

_____ My spouse and I communicate and react differently to the same experience. It used to annoy me, but now I see the beauty and genius of our differences.

_____ I am developing a new appreciation and capacity for humility, care, compassion, and gratitude in this relationship.

_____ I'm comfortable sleeping with my partner or on my own.

_____ Although the intensity has changed, I am more in love with my spouse now than I ever have been.

_____ It's nice to experience the wholeness of the relationship.

_____ Our sexual relationship is comfortable and enjoyable. There are times when it's not fulfilling, but it's nothing to worry about. It will be better next time.

_____ I sense that this relationship is helping me to become the best person I can be.

Note which areas contained the most 9s and 10s. This indicates the relational stage that you're currently in. If you see an equal number of 9s and 10s in a couple of stages, it means that you are probably in transition.

ABOUT THE AUTHORS

Pastor Kenneth Smith and co-pastor Tongela Smith are licensed and ordained ministers. Together, the Smiths founded and established Faith Works Christian Center, a non-denominational and multicultural church located in McDonough, Georgia.

Pastor Ken, originally from Buffalo, was born into a ministry family, the second son in a family of preachers. Pastor Ken has taught and counseled for more than 20 years, which has enabled him to reach many people with humor, warmth, and transparency.

As a child, Ken found his place in the music industry. In later years, Pastor Ken traveled the globe as a sought-after bass player for many national and international groups, choirs, and gospel artists. He finally settled into a ministry as a Worship/Music Arts Pastor for more than 10 years, and faithfully served in this capacity until answering the call as Senior Pastor of NDCC, alongside his beautiful wife, Tongela. Pastor Ken is a teacher by design and a true lover of God's word – a man who is resolute in his faith, and of fervent prayer. His love for God and God's people is evident. A quintessential family man, he possesses the gentleness and strength of an authentic servant leader. He is a man who has a pastor's heart.

Co-pastor Tongela D. Smith, Assistant Pastor of Faith Works Christian Center, has passionately answered the call to open minds and touch hearts with biblically based principles of inner healing and personal empowerment. Smith, of Niagara Falls, New York, was once a backup vocalist for James Brown, and a single mother struggling to discover her own identity. She admits that she learned some of life's most important lessons the hard way, but God stepped in and turned her misery into ministry.

Tongela combines her spiritual journey, leadership wisdom, and depth of spiritual understanding to help expose and shatter the forces that hold human souls captive. Her purpose is to empower people of all walks of life to break free from social, psychological, and physical limitations caused by toxic belief systems and the scars of life. Currently, Smith is the co-founder and CEO of New Direction Community Network Inc., a 501(c)3 non-profit agency established to provide mentoring and fostering of academic accomplishment, positive character development, healthy lifestyles, and leadership skills.

Tongela is also a Certified Life Coach and the CEO of IMPACT Life Coaching and Smith Mediation Services. She's a devout mother of four, mother-in-love of two, and grandmother of two.

Together, Ken and Tongela are committed to the vision of empowerment and the imparting of the global message of hope and faith into the lives of individuals around the world.

www.ingramcontent.com/pod-product-compliance
Lightning Source LLC
Chambersburg PA
CBHW072212270326
41930CB00011B/2619